Echoes Of Success

Taiwo Jacob

.

<u>Dedication</u>

I dedicate this book to the Almighty God who is the source of my inspiration, and who has made the publication of this work a success.

CONTENTS

PREFACE

It is a well known fact that things which are of less importance rarely attract people's attention and dedication. Thorns and briers do germinate at their own free cause, and no man would want to waste his precious time in tendering these plants of no value. But a garden of beautiful flowers, as well as a good tree of fortune demands that one cultivate the land for them, tender and keep them grown up so as to get their valuable result and reap their fruits later. Of course, success can likewise be likened to a good tree of fortune or a garden of beautiful flowers.

Success does not evolute, but one must work towards achieving it, although there is in every individual that in-built potential to excel. With personal efforts, determination, courage and faith in God, one will surely arrive at his desired habour of success safely. Moreover, achieving success and having the right state of mind; as an individual, a family or a group of people are things that cannot be obtained by living an isolated life. Hence, the need for good inter-personal relationships among people. But unfortunately these factors which are very important towards achieving breakthrough are what many people who even could have become geniuses in their various fields of life endeavour much lack in them.

Therefore, with the help of God who has endowed me with the inspiration and the ideas these are issues I seek to address in people's lives through this book. This book has been written in such a way that it is inspiring, motivational, instructional and thought provoking. In fact the book is very refreshing in its composition to arouse readers interest in reading through every verse and help them to derive those salient points of value embeded in it. Of course, these qualities and the other merits of this book make it readily acceptable to everyone.

I am of the strong belief that as you read through this book you will find it very useful. And you will come across those motivational words that will certainly move you into action, which, of course, will help you achieve your goals and desires in life.

T. O. Jacob

VERSES ON PRINCIPLE OF SUCCESS

1

He who fails to see himself very big despises the purpose for his creation.

2

Success can no one attain by treading the path of discouragement. Resolute mind conquers empires.

3

Most of those who soar high in business have once crawled under failure in trading.

4

The egg of success is hatched in the incubator of perseverance and courage.

5

One who is afraid of taking risks can never discover the secret of success.

6

Some people, of course, are born great, but every individual is created to be great.

7

Time is the process engine that needs to be filled with the raw materials of efforts to achieve the desire output of success.

8

He who cannot demarcate between capital and gain in business will soon root up the tree of fortune.

9

A man's greatest enemy of progress is the fear of failure within.

10

Risk taking is the genesis of success, but persistency is the medicine that cures failure.

11

Those that never imagine the beauty of walking in the skies never go beyond the roof.

12

Self restraint is an antidote for rash decision, indecision is a sure link to zero achievement.

13

Many fail to be the greatest because they lack what it takes to be great first.

14

He whose expectation is not greater than his needs has set a defective goal

15

Success is the easiest to accomplish of all tasks, but it has some deep rivers of challenges to cross enroute the bridge of faith and courage.

16

<u>Patience</u> is the cradle of <u>success,</u> and testimony is the crown of both.

17

One who is not endowed with initiatives cannot sail the boat of success.

18

Men of vision do talk less of failure

19

A projection is useless if it is bereaved of purpose.

20

He who does not execute his vision is worse than he who conceive none.

21

No one is without a talent, but many fail because they blindly encroach into the portion of others.

22

A faulty projection being chosen does wear out a team of competent executor.

23

Those who fail to think and plan for the future will later ponder over the past era of failures.

24

He who lacks perseverance in his field of endeavour will lack footprints of success to leave behind.

25

Success in making an accurate plan is like one building on a solid concrete of iron.

26

One who is ignorant of the gift God gave to him will soon experience the problem of an obsolete talent.

27

God has projected everyone great, but those who prefer seeing themselves as little as the ants are often the errand boys to slaves.

28

Wishes are the most painful if not translated into actions.

29

Those who have the fortitude to blow up the bridge of fear and doubt are the ones now walking on the river bank of success.

30

When there is the unity of purpose there will be a union of perfection.

31

God will show the way to the city of wealth, but man must take the great stride to the path of success.

32

Division gives birth to deadness of vision.

33

The beauty in success is hidden in the ability to hold it permanently

34

He who does not value the future cannot value planning.

35

A father who has successfully swum across the ocean of challenges will not be afraid to teach his boy the art of swimming in the stream of life experiences.

36

A man's special talent is God's inbuilt room of privacy for him.

37

Ability does not really lie in the strength to move mountains, it much lies in the power of conception of workable ideas.

38

One who spends his money on luxuries before earning it is the most unwise person among wasters.

39

He who has the desired qualities of leadership has the rod of control.

40

A producer of sub-standard product will surely project an ill of self.

41

The garment of impatience does deprive people the honour in service

42

Riches is like one drinking in the pool of honey, but no experience is as bitter as that of a person endowed with much experience of penury.

43

People rarely learn if there are no giant-like challenges to confront.

44

Those who sleep in the morning time of their lives do have the night hours of painful activities.

45

Those who have a sense of limitation suffer from the problem of crippled initiatives.

46

Walk along the field of honesty, then will you dig up the hidden gold of fortunes.

47

A lost property can one regain, a day lost can none recall. Therefore, waste not today.

48

Every disappointment of life does come along with some hidden opportunities.

49

Leadership does not go by age. After all, lion is not the biggest of animals yet he is crowned the king of the forest.

50

An impatient heart is a fertile soil where the seeds of failure and disappointment grow.

51

Those who entertain with their early days do play away their latter years.

52

Opportunity do comes to man unannouced, and it is those who watch for this hidden hour that do witness the dawn of success.

53

He who hates the sweat of labour will always eat the meal of shame.

54

A person that is dead is better than he who is still living and has built an empire of false hope surround self.

55

No rich can become richer without acquiring the coins of the poor, he needs exchanging the money of the poor for the goods of the rich.

56

The man whose wealth does not benefit his staff is a robber of labour.

57

The end of the darkest night of poverty is the bright shining morning of plenty.

58

A little child of vision will dictate the pace, and be a guiding shepherd to an empty adult who has none.

59

The solution to most of man's problems lives within himself.

60

He who only complains about the difficulties of life would waste much time in getting out of the land of problems.

61

A professor of wisdom who is still poor has not known the true meaning of prudence.

62

He who forcefully imposes himself on his colleagues must have seen some qualities in them which he has not.

63

Wealth has wings with which to fly, and it is very easy to tame with the knowledge of this.

64

Those who seek information are never starved of knowledge.

65

A product the maker cannot taste ought not to be taken to the market for test.

66

He who sows the seed of sleep will reap the fruit of penury.

67

One who only has the thoughts of pleasure in his head will incur many full days of wastages.

68

Do not force people to accept your good opinion, but let them first see the reason for a willing acceptance.

69

It is in confinement that a prudent heart is enlarged, in solitary it produces product of deep thought.

70

He who is careless with his health has many profitable hours to waste.

71

Ignorance is a terrible disease, enlightenment is the right medicine for is cure.

72

If nobody would feel the impact of you leaving an establishment, then your performance is below the tolerance level.

VERSES ON FAITH

73

Only faith in God can hatch the stony egg of impossibility to bring out the beautiful chick of riches.

74

Those who are ignorant of their right of kingship will be lost in the crowd.

75

Faith in God and faith in one's ability are two factors to a breakthrough in life.

76

Faith is the cord that pulls God's inexhaustible riches, but the opposite of it does bargain and settle for Satan's gifts.

77

To the faithless fellow is the word of Satan more powerful, weightier, and mightier than the unchanging promises of his Maker.

78

He who fails to earnestly plead with God for favour will in frustration talk to men for failure.

79

Faith is a conquering giant that conquers all other giants of evil.

80

Many days hunger vanishes with small morsel of meal.

81

The trial of faith is the temporal cloud in the sky of hope which dims the eyes against the moon of blessings.

82

All helps proceed from God, but He does make use of the men of love.

83

Faith is taller and fatter than fear, he who puts it on like a garment will overshadow all anxiety

84

Those who commit suicide do allow the cloud of doom to cover up their beautiful future ray of hope

85

He who debases himself will be served the meal of contempt

86

Mere shadow stands a terror to he who is a slave of fear.

87

Open your heart to God and become a conqueror in God, but expose it wide to men to become a captive of the godless.

88

He who would call to remembrance the past faithfulness of God will escape the present urge to doubt.

89

No captive is as great as one who is a captive of his own conscience.

90

Wisdom and folly are two parallel lines that can never meet, just as evil and failure cannot be attributed to God.

91

A king who does not know his own worth will often be seeing struggling with slaves for crumbs.

92

Worry means having faith in satan, and to be anxious is to have belief in his words.

93

The gift of God cannot be obtained by mere struggling. Faith is the thing that does the wonder.

94

Time is limited and precious, let them that use it use it wisely.

95

Today's pain is tomorrow's testimony, and tomorrow's victory is today's endurance.

VERSES ON FAMILY LIFE

96

A home where contentions exist is a little prison where failure is kept.

97

A father who lacks control over his child at home is under the control of an infant king.

98

Marriage is the union of two yoke bearers, but those who only regard it as a pleasurable ride cause it to fail.

99

The father of many wicked children has successfully built an empire for terror.

100

Wealth that has no portion of it spent on child's training is a wealth kept in trust for strangers.

101

He who keeps malice with his own child teaches him the basic rudiment of resentment.

102

A child that is kept from training is a child kept apart for sorrow.

103

A father of children who loves a child more than the others and makes a boast of it does invite trouble to the door steps of peace.

104

A husband who is still tied to the apron of his parents is an amateur in the midst of heads of families.

105

Love is very essential, and he who possesses it is endowed with a precious seed of peace.

106

The parents whose mouths are filled with the abusive language do have children whose mouths are "anointed" with volcanic words of cursing.

107

A father who sees his son revolt at home and would not talk acts a rebel sponsor who grooms a rebel leader in a peaceful nation.

108

We train children that we may have peace and joy. We leave them to their own ways to have pains and sorrow.

109

A child left untrained is a well set trap of anguish against the peace and souls of his parents.

110

He who curses his own parents has darkened his own days.

111

He who treats his wife like a little kid is still a child in application of wisdom

112

A wife that despises fidelity is a dent on the crown of her husband.

113

One who does not have time for the training of his children now will soon have decades of child trouble.

114

A wife who brings down showers of insult on her own husband in the presence of her daughter will groom a wife who rains down curses on the father-in-law in the presence of all.

115

The young shall grow: A father who teaches his little boy the rudiment of lying will soon have Mr. Falsehood living under his roof.

116

A good name is better than gold and silver. Nobody will be willing to name their child after Cain the murderer, neither will they be glad to have anyone decorate them with the initials of Judas Iscariot. Hence, he who names his own son after any man of terror has denied a child his fundamental human right.

117

Hoarders of bread do make their children's children refugees in their own land.

118

A mother who does every chore for her children indeed grooms a bunch of lazy and irresponsible team.

119

A parent who will not teach their children the courtesy of saying "thank you" has shut the door of favour against them.

VERSES ON GENERAL SOCIAL ISSUES

120

He who plants the grains of wickedness on the soil of evil invites the ravenous birds of disaster.

121

No sacrifice is without some elements of pains.

122

Character is not good enough if it has some elements of the bad in it.

123

The event of today is the history of tomorrow, hatred brought to life today shall give birth to tomorrow of discord.

124

He who insists to remain proud has his own rainbow consist of one colour.

125

Those who beat the drum of contention cannot escape hearing the echoes of it.

126

One who always provokes his friend to anger is an enemy in disguise.

127

He who loves encroaching into his neighbours' fields is of the generation of greedy dogs hunting for bones.

128

He who will not thank God for the gift of life will not be concerned if anybody loses his.

129

He who borrows and would not repay must have risen from the lineage of the ingrates.

130

No reply is as best as to give an arrogant fellow furious with raging words like being quiet in a gentle posture.

131

One who mourns when others rejoice, but would take many steps in dance when others wail, is wicked.

132

He who always guesses out other people's opinion has a seed of bias planted in his mind.

133

Love cannot be sweet if it is not enhanced with actions.

134

He who judges a matter before hearing from the parties to it is one who sows the seed of discord.

135

Those who never pass through the school of human experience do turn abusers of power when enthroned.

136

Hearing of truth is a whip of torment to he who defames the seal of sincerity.

137

What makes one a true friend to his friend is the ability to bear with him in the time of friction.

138

The easiest way into a man's heart is the lowly path of courtesy.

139

A man's true worth is reflected in the worth of his speech.

140

Love to be given out must have the attributes of such giving to self.

141

A deceiver has many of his victim's questions to answer with pretence.

142

A subject who strips a good king of his crown of royalty is an enemy of dignity.

143

He who refuses to accept correction has many more pits into which to fall.

144

One whom God gives the rain of riches is expected to sprinkle the dew of it on others.

145

A contentious fellow will refuse to buy peace even if sold for a penny.

146

Forgiveness means being able to receive an offence, and the ability not to retain it in the heart.

147

He who promotes the doctrine of tribalism and racial inequality will let loose the mad dog of violence and commotion.

148

Anyone who does much of face parade before a mirror has much ego to exhibit.

149

He who quickly admits his own error will have less insult to receive.

150

He who strips himself of the mantle of love will be clothed with the rag of hatred.

151

An offence forgiven fuels the fire of love, but many offences forgotten burn the seed of discord.

152

He who often suspects others of an evil deed needs suspect self of an evil thought.

153

Suspicion means looking at others with an eye void of love. It is to picture men with the mind of evil.

154

Forgiveness towards others is a mandatory price of love to be paid with God given currency of grace.

155

Destruction and pains are the two by-products from the raw material of an evil heart.

156

To treat a patient, one needs patience.

157

He who reveals the secret of his close friend acts a leaking basket with many holes.

158

A man of little words rarely has many people to offend.

159

Those who cook with the ingredients of conspiracy will eat the meal of discord.

160

He who talks carelessly has put on the face cap of shame.

161

One who only sees the beauty in self but none in others, is proud.

162

Hatred is a precious treasure to a wicked fellow, and a gossip cannot do without selling it to the human fowlers.

163

It is hatred that manufactures and packages murderous thought, before selling it to death.

164

He who wants prominence by all mean surely has many victims to trample on.

165

He who demands for his friend's eyes will be glad to have his enemy's head.

166

A gambler would gamble with money and property. But above all, he does gladly gamble with the future of his kids.

167

Those who carry the loads of others do carry them along with theirs with the mind of compassion.

168

He whose mindset is "if the hen breaks my pot, I will break her egg" is not a man of peace. He is ruled by the spirit of revenge, and firmly controlled by the demon of hatred.

169

He who calls his fellow man an ugly beast equally calls God an imperfect Maker.

170

Gossip is a demon which ruins one whom it rules.

171

He who uses God given resources to promote the cause of evil will have many converts won for Satan.

172

He who congregates with the fools shall be served the meals of error at the high table of deception.

173

One who takes wickedness as an acquaintance must have earlier nursed bitterness in the heart as a child.

174

The test of endurance is best observed when a man is greatly provoked.

175

He who escapes the trap of women will escape the terror of mind, and be a man of dignity.

176

A drunkard has some resemblance gene seen in an insane bull, and this is noticed in the display of little madness.

177

He who kills a fellow being also assassinates his own peaceful end.

178

Action reveals the real person in man.

179

He who hates God has murdered his own past, marred his present life, and also foolishly mortgages his future hope.

180

A child of a wealthy person who goes out begging for crumbs has not known the worth of his father.

181

Hatred is an expression of the bitterness in the heart.

182

He who offered a beggar the gift of a counterfeit currency is like a dry tree with no quality of a valuable fruit.

183

He who is placed on top cannot stand aloof, he needs to be supported by those who have their dwellings below the stool.

184

A song of melody out of the mouth of a man is always the most bitter rhyme in the ears of his enemies.

185

The demand of a foolish person is the greatest need in his eyes.

186

A person's character serves as a rally point that commands fortune or misfortune across his path.

187

Women of virtue never pretend their look.

188

Those who steal have grown eyelashes of greed.

189

He who harbours and keeps record of other people's offences for reference purposes shall be a perpetual slave of conscience.

190

Those who hunt down peace shall be hunted by the opposite of peace.

191

Love is not something to be imposed on the expected giver of it. It naturally flows from the pleasant fountain of affection.

192

He who does not see anything valuable in other people's ideas will remain a dwarf in understanding.

193

He who lacks respect for leadership cannot claim to have one for God.

194

Many who planted the trees of wickedness do not always live long enough to see their children, and children's children pluck their fruit of disaster to eat.

195

One who is angry for being helped will be mad for being loved.

196

He who will succeed in calling others to order must strip self of the unruly ego.

197

The heart that is always glad at seeing evil will be sad at seeing none.

198

The purported gesture of love from a deceptive fellow is nothing but a well decorated box of destruction.

199

Forgiveness is the end product of forbearance.

200

The knowledge one fails to impart into other people stands the risk of premature extinction.

201

Those who do not have a good case to present do pray for the rain of evil to fall.

202

An accused fellow who flees has indeed pronounced himself guilty.

203

Those who give out no love are the ones who most desire love.

204

A brutal fellow surrounds himself with the symbol of dangers.

205

The workers of darkness will be furious at the sight of the shining light of the moon.

206

The beginning of a fall is when one projects big the little self in him.

207

He who forgets his own needs to address the problems of others knows the secret of victory.

208

He who will give out the fruit of love must have earlier had the seed of it planted in him.

47

209

He who loves helping others builds a house of favour for his own children.

210

It is most impossible for anyone to deceive others, without first deceiving self at the time of scheming out the art of deception.

211

The mortal flesh has a terminal end, but no soul has a mortal element.

212

He who snubs at the king's counsel to be humble will soon be snubbed by the slaves in his own land.

213

Deception is the deep pit that swallows up men greedy of gains.

214

One who lacks respect for his boss should equally have no regard for promotion.

215

Were it not for the praise and flattery of men, no bad fellow would have grown wings to become a brutal monster.

216

He who loves sowing the seed of love and tolerance will soon have even his enemies fighting for him.

217

He who is of a biased mind will ruin a nation if made a people's judge.

218

Those who acquire wealth through shady deals do build with it great mansions of shadow.

219

A gossip has many stinking tales of death to spread.

THE BREAD OF AFFLICTION IS ALWAYS THE SWEETEST IN THE MOUTH OF A PAUPER, BUT HE WHO CONSIDERS THE EQUALITY OF MEN WILL HAVE PITY ON HIM.

SUCCESS IS LIKEA LADDER, IT HAS MANY RUNGS OF CHALLENGES.

THE THOUGHT OF FAILURE IN THE HEART IS THE SEEMINGLY INSIGNIFICANT ANT THAT DOES EASILY DESTROY THE HIDDEN GIANT OF SUCCESS IN MAN